Nature Meditations for Children

Written by Wyllow Elizabeth
Paintings by Kelly Foxton

With love to my children Cara, Brianna and Nicholas, and all the children from A.E.G.I.S. *-Wyllow Elizabeth*

For seekers of peace everywhere. *-Kelly Foxton*

ISBN 978-0-9939927-0-4

To order additional copies and for all other inquiries, please visit
www.naturebooks4kids.com
or write to wyllowweb@gmail.com

Introduction

Our world has changed so much in the past fifty years. As children, we roamed our neighbourhoods and played alone, and with friends, unsupervised. Today, children are bombarded by screens, organized activities, fears and too much information. It seems as though we want to rush our children into adulthood.

There are a number of things we can do to help slow this process down. Fresh air, simple routines, and time outdoors are a few of the things we can give our children to help them learn to take time for themselves and enjoy simple pleasures.

We can also teach them to meditate and in turn, to slow down for themselves. This will help them develop a rich inner world into which they can retreat and rejuvenate.

This book is a series of guided meditations, all of which have been tested and used with small groups and individual children.

As you read them aloud you will find you also benefit from accessing and developing **your** own "inner world". You may even find yourself bringing these images to mind during challenging times to help you "de-stress".

How to Use this Book

This book contains nine simple meditations. Children will find spirit guides and friends in their inner world as well as peace, joy and rejuvenation.

The first meditation is the easiest one – and after you have read it a few times you'll find yourself using it to "become grounded" during moments of stress and concern. Children will benefit from it helping them to calm themselves and move through the small difficulties that happen in life. It gets easier (and shorter – 1 to 2 minutes) to use with time and repetition.

The Spirit meditation occurs twice in this book – the first time it is an introduction to your heart garden. It is best if this meditation is experienced before the rest of the "heart garden" meditations. The second time it is worded as a reacquaintance with an old friend .

Children (and everyone) will benefit from repeating these meditations many times, so please use them over and over again.

You will find a 'notes' page after each meditation. It is my hope that you will use them to write your thoughts and ideas about what worked well, what didn't, and how you might add to or change the meditation so that it works for you and your children. Make it YOUR book. Feel free to add your ideas on how to change a meditation for your own use – maybe you will be inspired to add your own meditation.

Tree Meditation

Tree Meditation

I would like to share a story with you. You will draw the pictures in your mind. We will all hear the same words, but everyone's pictures are their very own.

It is time to get connected to the earth and sky so let's pretend we are trees...

Please close your eyes. Now imagine that you have tree roots growing out of the base of your spine and into Mother Earth. Feel them dig deep into the ground below you and find soft, cool energy that Mother Earth has waiting for you...

It feels nice to share this soft, cool energy from Mother Earth.

Now bring some of this peaceful energy from Mother Earth up out of the earth and into your body...

Up through your spine and feel it spread out - all through your body and expand out into the space around you, surrounding you with peaceful, cool energy...

Now out of the top of your head feel your branches grow up and away into Father Sky...

Feel your branches stretch and reach right up to the sky - feel the energy Father Sky has for you, warm and comforting...

Bring some of this light, warm energy down through your branches and into your body...

Fill up with this crystal energy from Father Sky, all through you and expanding out into your energy field...

Now we are connected between the worlds - we are in a sacred, magical place... You feel so much lighter now...

You can connect with the Earth and Sky anytime you want to. If you are feeling sad or excited or angry, getting a little of this energy will help you feel balanced again.

Let's hold this for just a minute... *(pause 3-5 minutes)*

When you are ready... Open your eyes...

Notes:

Spirit Meditation 1

Spirit Meditation 1

Today I want to take you to a special place inside of your heart... No one else can see into your heart this way, it is yours alone...

Close your eyes and feel your centre... Feel the ground below you and the air surrounding you... Feel the warmth of the Sun on your face...

Now imagine that you are walking up to a gate - maybe it is made of wood, or metal, maybe it is simple or fancy...

As you come to the gate, you notice a tree right beside it - this is your worry tree...

As you look closely at the tree you see a knot just where you can reach it...

Now you feel some ribbons in your hand - maybe only one or two, maybe a lot, you realize that there is a ribbon for each of the things you worry about - maybe how someone special in our family had an argument, maybe something a friend told you at school, maybe something you saw or heard that you don't quite understand, but it is making you feel anxious...

Any worry that you have in your heart is now held in your hand...

Put the ribbons on the knot and watch the tree absorb them... You feel the worries slipping out of you and into the tree - you can share your worries with your tree and you don't need to dwell on them so much... *(pause)*

You feel so much lighter now...

It is time to go into the garden...

Through the gate...

Look around - this is all yours - you can bring anything you want here - maybe you have a special friend here. I think you might see your friend now...

They're coming toward you in the most beautiful light...

You can see that your wise self looks like you, only a little bit older...

This is you in your wisest form - your wise self always knows the best thing for you to do - it always makes you feel happy to visit...

I will leave you now to visit with your wise self - to learn and play together. I know that your wise self will show you around your garden a little bit.

I will call you back in a little while.
(Pause approximately 2-5 minutes)

It is time to come back to us... Say goodbye to your higher self. Know that you will visit again soon...

Come back to the garden gate - and when you pass through it, you see a golden cloak on the worry tree...

Wrap yourself in the cloak and feel the soft warmth of it - this is special, just for you...

Walk back toward my voice...

And when you are ready, open your eyes...

Notes:

Spirit Meditation 2

Spirit Meditation 2

I am going to share another special story with you. Watch the pictures in your mind. Even though we all hear the same words, everyone's pictures are their very own - no two people see them alike.

Please close your eyes.

Now I want to take you to your special place inside of your heart...

No one else can see into your heart in this way, it is yours alone.

You are walking up to your gate... As you come to the gate you see your worry tree...

You see a knot just where you can easily reach it...

Can you feel the ribbons in your hand? - Maybe only one or two, maybe a lot. There is a ribbon for each of the things you worry about...

Put the ribbons on the knot and the tree will absorb them - now you can share your worries with your tree and you don't need to dwell on them so much...

(Pause)

You feel so much lighter now... It is time to go into the garden... Through the gate...

You feel so much lighter now... It is time to go into the garden... Through the gate...

Look around - this is all yours - you can bring anything you want here - this time you'll visit your wise self again...

There, coming toward you is the most beautiful light...

You can see your wise self. Now is your chance to share a story, a concern, or to learn and play together. Your wise self always knows the best thing for you to do.

I will leave you now to visit with your wise self, it always makes you feel happy to be here...

I know that your wisest self enjoys telling you new stories about your life and future. I will call you back in a little while...
(Pause approximately 2-5 minutes)

It is time to come back to us...

Say goodbye to your wise self - Know that you can visit any time you want to...

Let's return to the garden gate - and when you pass through it, you see your golden cloak on the worry tree...

Wrap yourself in the cloak and feel the soft warmth of it...

Now walk back toward my voice... And when you are ready open you eyes...

Notes:

Root Child Meditation

Root Child Meditation

I am here to share another story with you. Again you will draw the pictures in your mind. We will all hear the same words, but everyone's pictures are their very own.

Please close your eyes. It is time to visit your special place inside of your heart... Take some deep breaths to find your centre... Your place of balance...

It is a wonderful day to meander down the lovely path to your garden gate... Take a moment to enjoy the beauty that surrounds you...

See your gate... As you come to the gate you notice your worry tree seems so very happy to see you... You are such good friends...

Look closely at the tree for your knot...

Gather together your ribbons – maybe only one or two, maybe a lot, there is a ribbon for each of the things that you worry about – maybe one is for a disagreement your heard on the playground, maybe one is for your friend who is feeling ill, the ribbons represent things that are making you feel anxious...

Whatever your worries are it is time to share them with your tree...

As you put the ribbons on the knot your tree absorbs them – now you can share your worries with your tree and you don't need to dwell on them so much...

You feel so much more relaxed and calm...

It is time to go into the garden...

Through the gate...

On this visit you are meeting a very shy friend... So be as quiet as a mouse and look around you very carefully... This friend is very difficult to see... Oh, do you feel that tap on your leg? Look down – do you see that very dirty, tiny little root child?

This friend is going to share something very special with you... Feel yourself shrinking and slipping into the ground... As you shrink and slip down notice that you are changing into a seed...

Now you are planted in the ground, your new friend will share with you how to grow from this tiny seed into a beautiful plant... Will you be a flower or a tomato plant, a bush or a tree?

I will leave you now to transform into the magnificent plant that you are about to discover...

It is time to learn about this growing part of yourself – more things in your heart garden to try, here in your inner world...

I will call you back soon... *(Pause approximately 2 – 5 minutes)*

It is time to return to me... Slowly, slowly transform back into the wonderful child of the earth that you are... Thank your Root Child friend – I know that you will visit with this friend, and become a plant many, many times...

Come back to the garden gate. Collect your brown and green cloak ~ doesn't it smell earthy? Wrap yourself in the cloak and feel warm and soothed by it – what a nice feeling...

Walk back to my voice... *(Pause a few seconds...)*

And when you are ready, open your eyes...

Notes:

_____

_____

_____

_____

_____

_____

_____

_____

_____

_____

_____

_____

_____

_____

_____

_____

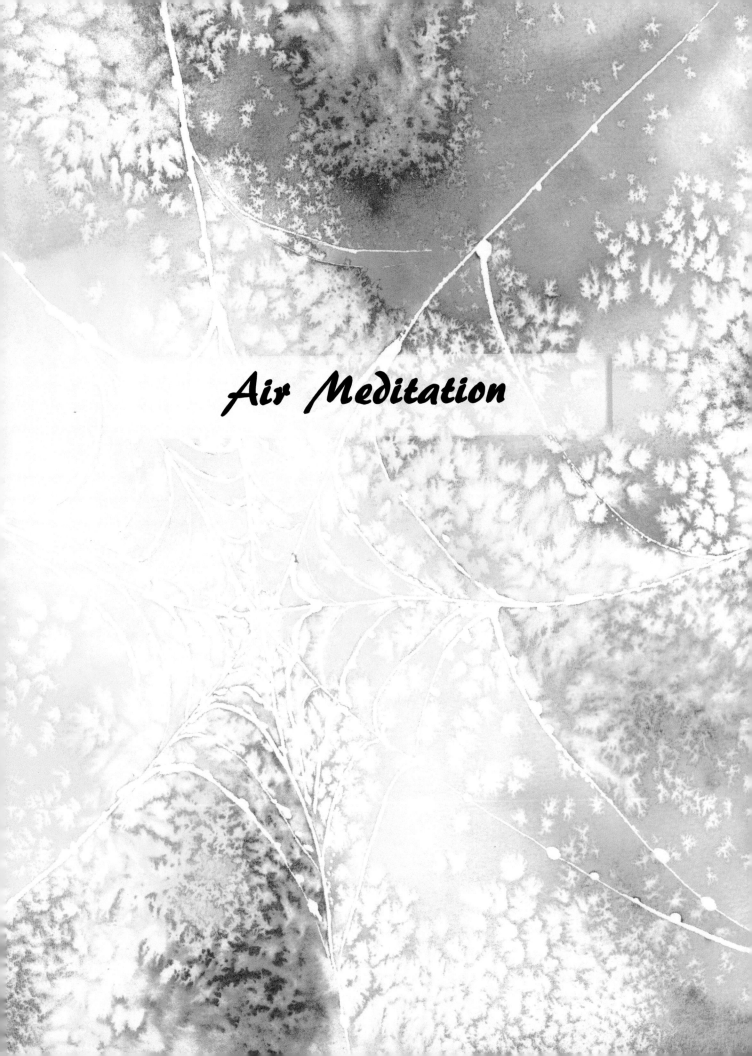

Air Meditation

Air Meditation

I am here to tell you a new story. Once more you will draw the pictures in your mind. And we will all hear the same words, but everyone's pictures are their very own.

Please close your eyes. I want you to go to your special place inside of your heart...

See your gate... As you come to the gate, notice your worry tree...

Look closely at the tree for your knot...

Now feel your ribbons in your hand - maybe only one or two, maybe a lot, there is a ribbon for each of the things that you worry about - maybe you had an argument with a friend, maybe you saw or heard something that you don't quite understand, but it is making you feel anxious...

Whatever your worries are, it is time to share them with your tree...

Put the ribbons on the knot and the tree absorbs them - now you can share your worries with your tree and you don't need to dwell on them so much...

You feel so much more relaxed now...

It is time to go into the garden...

Through the gate...

The special friend that you meet is a Fairy, an air spirit... Your Fairy friend is very small - she fits into your hand...

As your new friend flutters beside you, you notice that you are fluttering too... You have little wings here in your garden this time!

Flutter along with your Fairy friend and see a new part of your garden - a tree house!

It is time to discover this airy part of yourself. There are more things in your heart garden to learn about in your inner world...

I will call you back soon... *(Pause approximately 2-5 minutes)*

It is time to come back... Say goodbye to your Fairy friend . Know that you will visit with this friend many times...

Return to the garden gate - and when you pass through it, you see your golden cloak on your worry tree... Wrap yourself in the cloak and feel warm and soothed, what a nice feeling...

Walk back ... *(Pause a few seconds...)*

And when you are ready, open your eyes...

Notes:

_____

_____

_____

_____

_____

_____

_____

_____

_____

_____

_____

_____

_____

_____

_____

_____

_____

Star Child Meditation

Star Child Meditation

I want to share another story with you. It is time for you to imagine all of the beautiful pictures in your mind.

Please close your eyes... It is time to visit your special place inside of your heart... Take a big, deep breath and gently let it out... *(Pause)*

And another deep breath... and one more...

Now walk down the path toward your heart garden, isn't it a nice walk? Look around you... Do you see that bird flying right in front of you?

Look, there is your gate... Your worry tree seems so happy to see you...

Look closely at the tree for your knot...

Do you have many ribbons in your hand? – There is a ribbon for each of the things that you worry about – maybe you are concerned about a loved one who is not feeling well, maybe you told a falsehood and are worried about how everyone will feel when they find out, perhaps something is making you feel anxious...

Whatever your worries are it is time to share them with your tree...

Put the ribbons on the knot and watch the tree absorb them – now you can share your worries with your tree and you don't need to dwell on them so much...

You feel so light and relaxed...

It is time to go into the garden...

Through the gate...

This time there is a very bright, shimmering and shining visitor waiting for you... Hold hands with your new friend... Do you feel yourself floating? Up and up, higher and higher... Right up to the sky... You are surrounded by stars and oh! My, it looks like your friend is a star too... This is your very own star – born at the very moment you were born, connected to you by the universe... You are part of each other...

It is time for you to have a nice visit with your star and see all that the universe has in store for you...

I know that some of the other star children are excited to see you visiting here... Have a lovely time visiting with all of the star children...

I will call you home soon...

(Pause approximately 2 – 5 minutes)

It is time to return to me... Give your Star Child a big hug and thank them for sharing this time with you – Know that you can visit with this friend whenever you wish...

You may wish to visit here for guidance and loving support whenever you feel alone or unsure...

Return to me at the garden gate. When you pass through it, collect your star-covered cloak from your worry tree... Wrap yourself in the cloak and feel nice and cozy – what a lovely feeling...

Come back to my voice... *(Pause a few seconds…)*

And when you are ready open your eyes...

Notes:

Fire Meditation

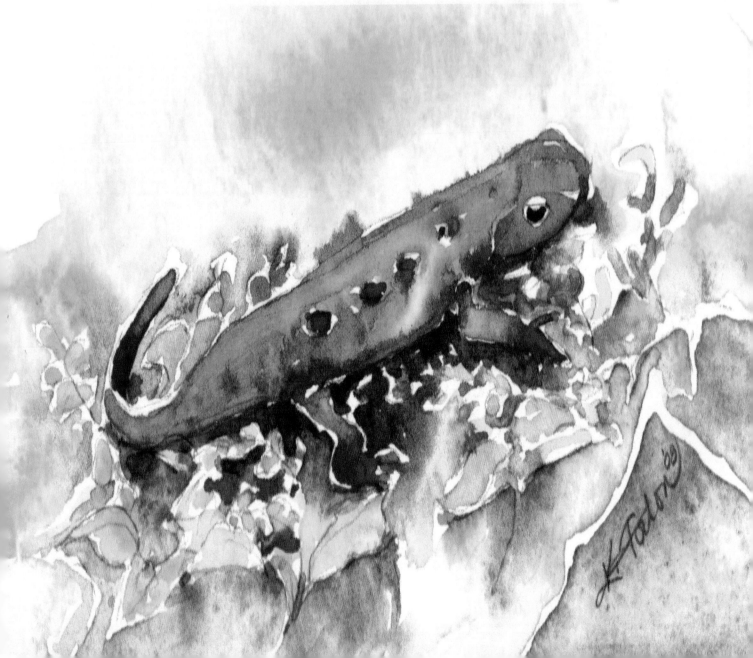

Fire Meditation

I am going to tell you another story… Once again the pictures for this story are in your very own mind… You have such a wonderful imagination…

It is time to feel connected to the earth and sky so let's pretend we are trees for a moment…

Now we are connected between the worlds - we are in a sacred, magical place… *(Pause)*

Now I want you to go to your special place inside of your heart… See your gate…

Come up to your worry tree…

Leave your worry ribbons on the special knot.

There is a ribbon for each of the things you worry about - maybe you did something by accident and don't want to be in trouble, maybe you had a bad dream and you feel anxious… Whatever your worries are it is time to share them with your tree…

Put the ribbons on the knot so the tree can absorb them – your tree is so magical, it turns your worries into flowers for your garden! You can let your worries go…

You feel so much lighter now…

It is time to go into the garden…

Through the gate…

A new special friend is waiting for you in your garden – this friend is a Dragon, a fire Spirit…

Your Dragon can fly! You can climb on his back and go with him…

Your Dragon wants to show you your garden from up high and makes you feel safe when you are flying together…

You feel so calm and peaceful up on his back…

Go with him and see this new view of your garden… As you fly you notice a fire pit down below, look, you are going to visit lots of friends at the fire pit…

Time to learn about this fiery part of yourself… Remember? Everything here in your heart garden is about you… I will call you back soon…

(Pause approximately 2-5 minutes)

It is time to come back…

Say goodbye to your Dragon friend, know that you can visit with him whenever you want to…

Come back through the garden gate - when you pass through it, wrap yourself in your red, fiery cloak - you feel so soft and warm - what a lovely feeling…

Walk back toward my voice… *(Pause a few seconds…)*

And when you are ready, open your eyes.

Notes:

Water Meditation

Water Meditation

Here is another special story. Are you ready for the pictures you have drawn in your mind?

Listen and hear the same words, but know that your pictures are your very own.

Let's go to your special place inside your heart...

See your gate...

As you come to the gate, you notice a tree beside it - this is your worry tree...

As you look closely at the tree, you see a knot just where you can reach it...

Now you feel some ribbons in your hand - maybe only one or two, maybe a lot. You are holding a ribbon for each of the things you worry about - maybe a friend said an unkind thing, maybe you are worried that someone is not going to be your friend anymore...

Whatever your worries are, it is time to share them with your tree...

Put the ribbons on the knot and the tree absorbs them - now you can share your worries with your tree... *(Pause)*

You feel so much lighter now...

It is time to go into the garden...

Through the gate...

Now you are going to a new place in your garden - as you walk a bit you find a stream...

This stream is very special - the water looks like flowing rainbows...

There is someone swimming toward you in the water...

This new friend is part person and part fish!

You swim with your mer-friend in the rainbow stream. It feels very relaxing and cool in the water, any cuts or bruises you have are feeling better just by being here in your stream...

Take a few minutes to discover this watery part of yourself...

I will call you back soon.

(Pause approximately 2-5 minutes)

It is time to come back...

Say goodbye to your mer-friend - Know that you can visit whenever you want to...
You will want to visit this stream for healing when you are hurt...

Come back through the garden gate. When you have passed through it, dry yourself off with your soft, blue cloak from your worry tree...

Wrap yourself up and feel all warm and comfy in it - what a beautiful feeling...

Walk back toward my voice... *(Pause a few seconds...)*

And when you are ready, open your eyes...

Notes:

Earth Meditation

Earth Meditation

I want to share another story with you. It is time for you to imagine all of the beautiful pictures in your mind.   You imagine such amazing pictures …

It is time to go to your special place inside your heart…

See your gate …

As you come to the gate, you notice your worry tree …

There is the knot, just where you can reach it …

Feel your ribbons in your hand. There is a ribbon for each of the things you worry about: maybe someone said something that hurt your feelings, maybe you heard a family member argue …

Whatever your worries are, it is time to share them with your tree …

Put the ribbons on the knot, the tree absorbs them. Now you have shared your worries with your tree and you don't need to dwell on them so much …

You feel so much lighter now …

It is time to go into the garden …

Pass through the gate …

This very special friend is a Gnome, an earth spirit …

This Gnome is a little smaller than a toddling baby and is wearing a long red hat.

This new friend wants to show you something special - so special I don't even know what it is …

Go with him or her and see a new corner of your garden …

I will leave you to discover this earthy part about yourself - everything here in your heart garden is about you, it is your inner world …

I will call you back soon …

(*Pause approximately 2-5 minutes*)

It is time to come back …

Say goodbye to your Gnome friend - know that you can visit whenever you want to …

Come back to the garden gate - and when you pass through it, you see your golden cloak on your worry tree …

Wrap yourself in the cloak and feel warm and soothed by it - what a nice feeling …

Walk back toward me … *(Pause a few seconds…)*

And when you are ready, open your eyes …

Notes:

About the Author...

Wyllow Elizabeth was raised in Ontario and now lives in the Annapolis Valley, Nova Scotia with her three children. She has loved working as a childcare provider, workshop facilitator and foster parent.

a

Sharing her deep understanding of nature's restorative healing power with children has been a life long dream.

"Nature Meditations for Children" is her first book.

About the Artist...

Kelly Foxton is best known for her work as a wildlife artist, art teacher, and author/illustrator of her first children's book titled "Mother Nature Knows..."

She lives in Bear River, Nova Scotia with her husband and three children.

Inspired by the natural beauty of Bear River and surrounding areas, Kelly creates art as a tribute to our Mother Earth and the many faces of Her Children.

To view more artwork by Kelly Foxton please visit
www.kellyfoxtonartist.vpweb.com

Nature Books for Kids publishes and distributes a collection of exclusive, nature-based children's literature written by talented, up and coming Canadian authors.

For submission inquiries and information about books published by Nature Books for Kids, please visit our website

www.naturebooks4kids.com

Made in the USA
Charleston, SC
16 July 2016